D1713316

HOW TO DRAW

the Meanest, Most Terrifying

MONSTERS

CAPSTONE PRESS
a capstone imprint

Velocity is published by Capstone Press,
1710 Roe Crest Drive, North Mankato, Minnesota 56003.
www.capstonepub.com

 Books published by Capstone Press are manufactured with paper
containing at least 10 percent post-consumer waste.

Library of Congress Cataloging-in-Publication Data
How to draw the meanest, most terrifying monsters / by Mike Nash ... [et al.].
    p. cm.—(Velocity. Drawing)
Includes bibliographical references.
Summary: "Provides step-by-step instructions for how to draw monsters"—Provided by
publisher.
ISBN 978-1-4296-7538-3 (library binding)
1. Monsters in art—Juvenile literature. 2. Drawing—Technique—Juvenile literature.
I. Nash, Mike (Mike Howard)
NC825.M6H69 2012
743'.87—dc23

           2011041121

Illustrators
Mike Nash
Carlo Molinari
Martin Bustamante
Matt Edwards

Editorial Credits
Veronica Correia, designer; Nathan Gassman, art director; Laura Manthe,
    production specialist

Artistic Effects
Shutterstock: David M. Schrader (background)

Printed in the United States of America in Stevens Point, Wisconsin.
102011   006404WZS12

MONSTER MANIA

Monsters with multiple heads. Slimy sea creatures from the watery depths. Monster aliens with massive tentacles. Whatever your favorite monsters are you'll soon be bringing them to life on paper. Sharpen your pencil, and let's get started!

TABLE OF CONTENTS

Flying Gargoyle

GARGOYLES AREN'T SUPPOSED TO BE CUTE,
ESPECIALLY NOT THIS WINGED TERROR. PLACING
THE GARGOYLE AT THE EDGE OF THE BUILDING
GIVES PROPORTION TO THE DRAWING.

1. Using two colors (pink and blue), draw wire frames for the figure and the building.

2. Carefully draw tubes over the gargoyle's wire frame. Keep in mind the angle you are viewing it from.

3. Sketch in the details and add the building over the perspective lines.

4. Ink the drawing for a cleaner scene.

5. Color to showcase the weather and time of day.

FACT: Gargoyle structures were originally designed as spouts on buildings. The spouts threw rainwater away from the buildings to prevent damage.

SWAMP BEAST

DON'T GET TOO CLOSE TO THE WATER'S EDGE! WITH GLOWING EYES AND RAZOR-SHARP CLAWS, THIS BEAST MEANS BUSINESS.

FACT: Stories of swamp beasts are less popular than sea monster stories. But a swamp monster called the Skunk Ape is said to live in swamps in the southeastern United States.

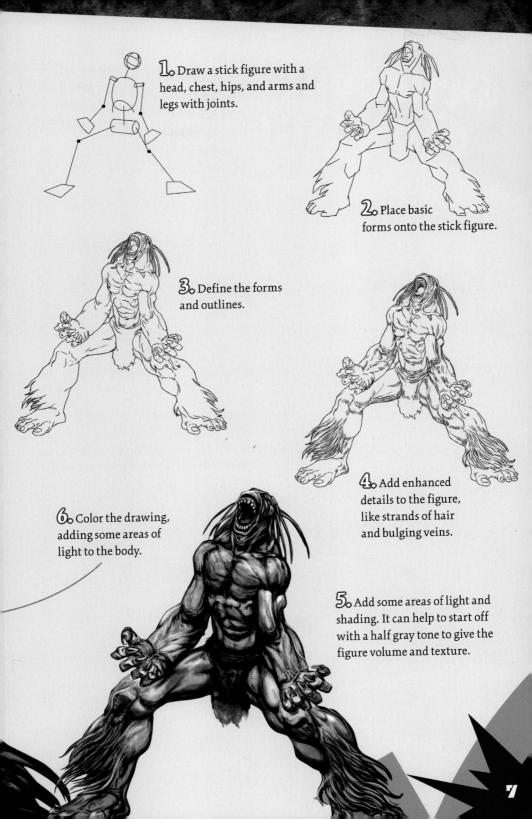

1. Draw a stick figure with a head, chest, hips, and arms and legs with joints.

2. Place basic forms onto the stick figure.

3. Define the forms and outlines.

4. Add enhanced details to the figure, like strands of hair and bulging veins.

6. Color the drawing, adding some areas of light to the body.

5. Add some areas of light and shading. It can help to start off with a half gray tone to give the figure volume and texture.

Gruesome Gorgon

IN GREEK MYTHS, LOOKING AT GORGONS COULD TURN PEOPLE TO STONE. IT'S EASY TO SEE WHY! DRAWING THE MANY SNAKES AT DIFFERENT ANGLES WILL HELP YOU FOCUS ON DETAILS.

1. Draw a skeleton of the gorgon. Use one color for the head, arms, and upper parts of the body. Use another color for the legs.

2. Over your skeleton draw in basic tubes and curves to give the gorgon a twisted shape. Add guidelines for the snakes. These guidelines will help you remember the direction and flow of each one.

3. Define the twisted mass, adding a bit of depth to the darkest areas.

4. Ink over the top and add shading to give the drawing depth. Don't forget to let the monster's eyes shine out!

5. Finish your drawing with colors of your choice. And remember not to look into those eyes!

BANSHEE

BEWARE THE SHRIEK OF THE BANSHEE! IN IRISH LEGENDS, THE CRY OF ONE OF THESE WOMEN MEANT THAT SOMEONE WAS ABOUT TO DIE. DRAWING THIS SHADOWY FIGURE WILL HELP YOU MASTER LIGHTING AND CONTRAST.

1. Make a skeleton that shows the basic shape and direction the figure will take.

2. Fill out the body and make a frame for the hair and the ball of light.

3. Add details. Use curved lines on the dress to give it shape and show movement.

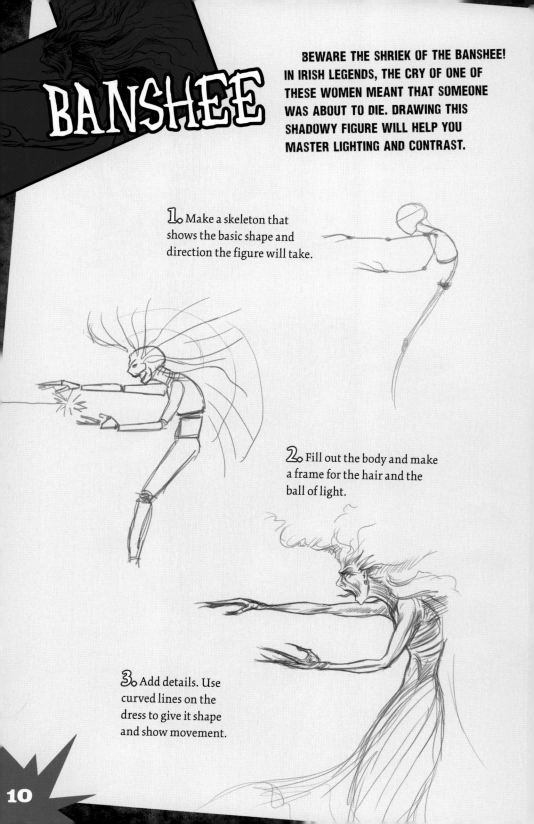

4. Darken areas at the back of the body and other shadowed parts. Start adding flowing lines to the hair.

5. Add color and fill in details. Make sure to remember where the ball of light is shining from.

FACT: According to legends, banshees could appear in human or animal form.

ARACHNE

DON'T GET CAUGHT IN THIS SPIDER'S WEB! WITH KILLER CLAWS AND EIGHT POWERFUL LEGS, THIS ANGRY ARACHNID IS THE STUFF OF NIGHTMARES.

1. Make a skeleton. Use balls to show joints in the skeleton, **cylinders** to show limbs, and ovals for the hips and torso. A cross helps define the center of the face and which direction the spider is looking.

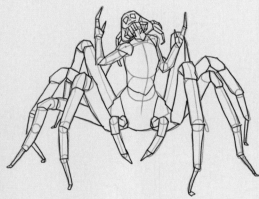

2. Use straight lines to start connecting the joints and limbs together. **Perspective** is important. Make sure each leg and its position can be understood in relation to the others. Start with the front legs and work backward. When placing legs behind others, overlap the legs to avoid confusion.

3. Remove unnecessary structure lines. Add hairs, spots, and lumps to the skin. Use lines around the joints to suggest folded skin and bony knees. Lengthen the front claws.

FACT: All spiders are classified as arachnids. Other members of this group include ticks, mites, and scorpions. All arachnids have two main parts and are wingless.

4. Shade your monster. Here the light is coming from above, with shadows underneath. Focus on trying to give the body a **three-dimensional** appearance. Add a floor and a shadow cast by the monster.

5. The use of red and pink around the mouth and arms helps draw attention to the face. Use strong highlights on the fangs and eyes to make them look wet and contrast with the dry wiry hair. Tiny hooks on the tips of the claws and fangs suggest that the monster uses poison to catch its victims.

cylinder—a shape with flat, circular ends and sides shaped like the outside of a tube
perspective—making distant objects smaller than nearer ones so the view looks as someone would see it
three-dimensional—having length, width, and height

CENTAUR

CENTAURS WERE KNOWN FOR THEIR UNRULY WAYS IN GREEK MYTHS. IF YOU SEE ONE OF THESE CREATURES COMING TOWARD YOU, GET OUT OF THE WAY!

1. This monster combines parts of a horse and a man. Use balls to show joints in the skeleton. Use cylinders to show limbs and ovals for the hips and torso. Horses have large shoulder and thigh muscles. Show these muscles with large oval shapes and a central line to show the leg direction.

2. Start connecting the body parts together with straight lines. The front legs of a horse work in a similar way to people's legs, with a form of hip, knee, and ankle joints. Pose the horse's front legs as though they were an extension of the man's body. This will help the transition between man and horse blend more naturally.

3. Smooth out your lines and focus on capturing a strong muscular shape. Begin to add definition to the torso, facial features, and fingers. Note how the pose flows in a circular motion across the back, up the torso, and down the arms and ax to meet the tail. This flow creates a pose full of movement and energy.

4. Refine the limbs and think of how the muscles would flex and stretch. Note how the muscles of the man's lower stomach can merge easily into the horse's chest and shoulder. A seamless connection that isn't too thin at the waist makes a better image.

5. Here the light is coming from above, with shadows underneath. Consider the angle of the limbs and how intensely the light source would be lighting their various sides. Note how the arm muscle is being squashed against the chest and the area of shadow this creates. Add stress lines to the back of the hands and fingers to show that the ax is being gripped tightly.

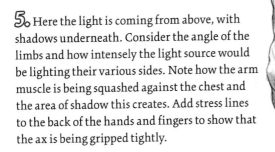

6. Decide on coat color and leg markings. Choose the same color for the hair and tail to help link the two halves of the monster. Blend the skin color into the fur gently. A sudden transition could look awkward. Add dark shadows and small highlights to muscle creases to suggest skin shine and increase depth.

EVIL OCTOPUS

THIS MONSTROUS OCTOPUS IS ON THE HUNT. NOT EVEN THE BIGGEST SHIPS CAN ESCAPE ITS FIRM GRIP.

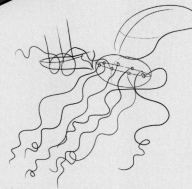

1. Draw a bean shape for the octopus' head. Then draw the oval shape of the body. Draw another oval inside the first one. Mark eight points on the second oval. From these points, draw the guidelines for the eight tentacles. Frame the ship's hull with its three **masts**.

2. Draw the eye, mouth, and horns on the head. Shape and taper the tentacles and add detail to the ship.

3. Draw the suckers on the bottom of the tentacles in two rows. Start drawing the lines in the ship's wooden hull, and draw small oval shapes for the sharks.

FACT: The giant Pacific octopus is the largest type of octopus. The largest one on record weighed more than 600 pounds (272 kilograms).

5. Add shadows at the bottom and on the right side of all the elements with black or another dark color. At the front, use light shades or white. Use pure white for the light on the tentacles to make the monster's skin shine.

4. Finish coloring, making stripes on the octopus' tentacles and head.

mast—a tall pole on a ship's deck that holds its sails

MinotAur

1. Draw the guidelines for all parts of the body.

2. Draw the shapes of the body on the guidelines. Give form to a muscular chest, shoulders, and arms. Draw the eyes and the base of the nose.

3. Add details, including the fur, hooves, toes, and mouth.

4. Continue adding details.

5. Use a separate color to mark the furry areas of the body.

6. Add shadows at the bottom of various body parts using a darker shade of the colors used or with black. Finally, add light areas with lighter shades of the same color or white.

ALIEN SLUG

WITH ITS GAPING MOUTH, THIS SNAIL-LIKE ALIEN BEAST COULD SCARE AWAY EVEN THE BRAVEST ENEMY. A GREAT EXAMPLE OF SCALE, THE TINY SPACEMEN SHOWCASE THE MONSTER'S ENORMOUS SIZE.

1. Use a simple rising tube shape as a basic structure for the slug.

2. Break the tube into sections, and start shaping the body parts.

3. Add in the tentacles, mouth parts, body muscles, and other details.

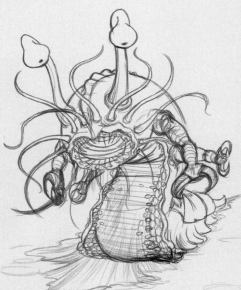

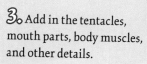

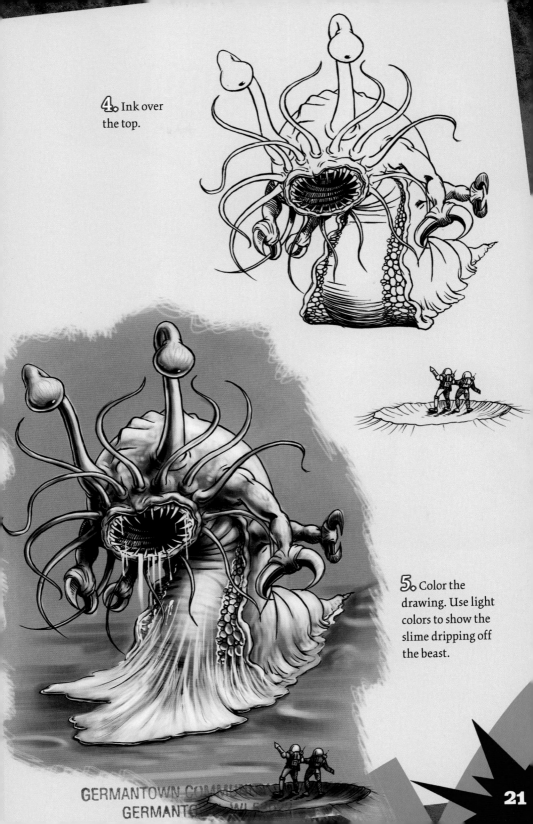

4. Ink over the top.

5. Color the drawing. Use light colors to show the slime dripping off the beast.

Monster Dragon

DON'T MAKE THIS DRAGON ANGRY! IT'S LOOKING TO PICK A FIGHT, AND ITS SHARP CLAWS, POWERFUL TAIL, AND MANY TEETH ARE SURE TO BE ADVANTAGES!

1. Draw a skeleton with a head, neck, chest, hips, and limbs with joints.

4. Shade to give the figure volume and texture.

5. Color the dragon, adding a few more areas of lighting to complete.

FACT: Not all myths feature destructive dragons. Chinese myths often include friendly dragons that bring good fortune.

3. Define the forms and outlines by adding details to the figure.

2. Place basic forms onto the skeleton using straight thin lines.

RAMPAGING REPTILIAN

THIS SCALY BEAST LEAVES BEHIND A PATH OF DESTRUCTION WHEREVER HE GOES. THE SHADOW THE BEAST CASTS ADDS TO THE DRAWING'S THREATENING FEEL.

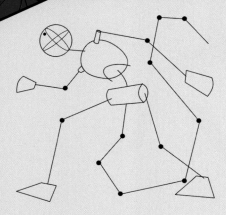

1. Draw a skeleton. Use a cylinder for the lower body and an oval-like shape for the upper body.

2. Place basic forms on to the stick figure using straight lines. Remove unnecessary lines.

3. Define the forms and outlines to create a more complex figure.

4. Add details, including the tail scales and chest muscles.

5. Shade the figure, adding areas of light and shadow.

6. Color the monster and add areas of light to the tail and the monster's left arm. Don't forget to draw the beast's looming shadow.

RAGING WARRIOR

THE MANY LIMBS AND BULKY MUSCLES OF THIS WARRIOR GIVE IT AN EDGE IN BATTLE. IF THAT'S NOT ENOUGH TO SCARE ENEMIES AWAY, IT CAN BARE ITS RAZOR-SHARP TEETH.

1. Draw a skeleton, using a circle for the torso and a rectangle for the hips.

2. Form the basic shapes of the body parts and the sword.

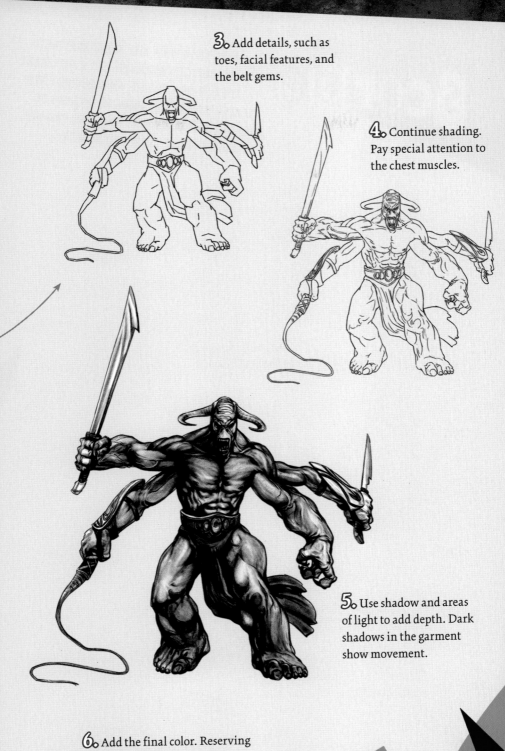

3. Add details, such as toes, facial features, and the belt gems.

4. Continue shading. Pay special attention to the chest muscles.

5. Use shadow and areas of light to add depth. Dark shadows in the garment show movement.

6. Add the final color. Reserving bright colors for the belt and garment draw attention to the monster's midsection.

scorpio

MOST SCORPIONS KILL THEIR PREY WITH POISON, BUT THIS MONSTER HAS A DIFFERENT WEAPON. IT CAN CREATE AN ELECTRIC FIELD TO KEEP ATTACKERS AWAY. IF ENEMIES DO GET CLOSE ENOUGH, THIS MONSTER CAN USE ITS SHARP FRONT CLAWS TO ATTACK.

1. Draw a skeleton with two front claws and eight legs.

2. Give basic shapes to the body parts.

3. Add details, including the chest muscles and facial features.

4. Continue filling in the detail for the claws, tail, and other parts.

5. Shade the figure.

6. Add color. Use a light yellow on the inside edges of certain body parts so the monster looks electrified.

SNAKOSAUR

NO ENEMY STANDS A CHANCE AGAINST THIS TRIPLE THREAT. WITH THE SPEED OF A LION, THE ABILITY TO SOAR, AND THREE FIRE-BREATHING REPTILIAN HEADS, SNAKOSAUR ALMOST ALWAYS CLAIMS VICTORY.

1. Draw the guidelines of the monster's body, tail, limbs, heads, and wings. Use oval shapes for the heads, chest, and pelvis.

2. Form the shapes of the body parts.

3. Add details, such as neck fur, claws, and the three rows of feathers on the wings.

4. Continue adding details, paying special attention to the feathers and fur to show their irregularities.

5. Color all the body parts.

6. Add shadows and areas of light on the monster. Fill in the details on the rock cliff.

Boggit

THIS TROLL-LIKE MONSTER HIDES IN BOGS, WAITING FOR ITS NEXT VICTIM. ONCE HE SNATCHES A MEAL, HE DOESN'T LET A BIT GO TO WASTE.

1. Draw the body frame in two sections. It should look like deflated balloons on top of each other. Add an oval shape for the head.

2. Add tubes for legs and arms.

3. Add more details, such as the warts and drool. Draw hair at random spots all over the body.

4. Ink over the top.

5. A light green-yellow color creates this monster's gross, sickening look. Add light areas on the monster's lower body to indicate a light source shining from the monster's left side.

Troglodyte

STAYING AWAY FROM THE WATER WON'T
KEEP YOU SAFE FROM THIS BULGING BEAST.
THE AMPHIBIAN ROAMS LAND LOOKING
FOR VICTIMS TOO. THIS DRAWING
HELPS GIVE THE FEELING THAT THE
MONSTER IS FLOATING IN WATER.

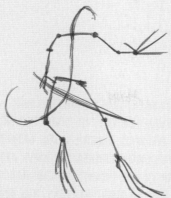

1. Wire-frame the figure, making sure to keep everything flowing.

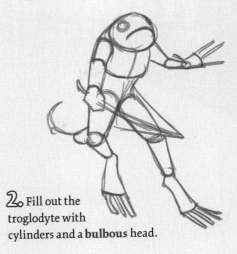

2. Fill out the troglodyte with cylinders and a **bulbous** head.

3. Add details, making sure everything has a feel of floating.

4. Ink over.

5. When adding the color, get some reference images of underwater animals to help with the unusual lighting.

bulbous—resembling a bulb, especially in roundness

Frankenstein's MONSTER

FRANKENSTEIN'S MONSTER HAS SURVIVED THE TEST OF TIME. BUT HE ISN'T WITHOUT WORRIES. THE MONSTER HAS RECENTLY BROKEN HIS ARM. AFTER A TRIP TO THE GRAVEYARD, HE HAS A NEW ONE TO MAKE REPAIRS. BUT WILL HIS REPAIRS WORK?

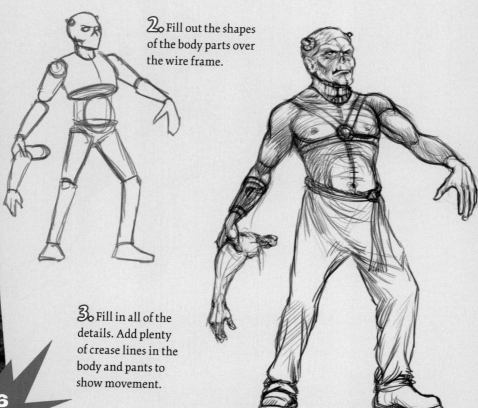

1. Draw a wire frame, using a triangle for the monster's hips.

2. Fill out the shapes of the body parts over the wire frame.

3. Fill in all of the details. Add plenty of crease lines in the body and pants to show movement.

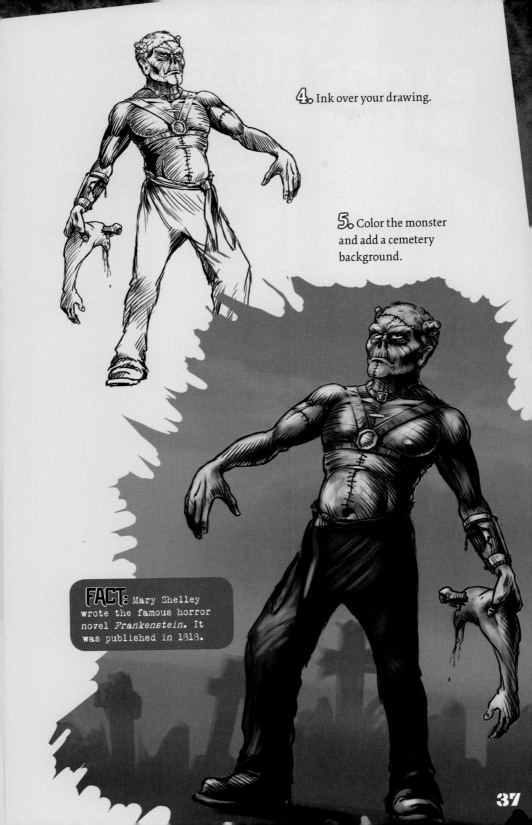

4. Ink over your drawing.

5. Color the monster and add a cemetery background.

FACT: Mary Shelley wrote the famous horror novel *Frankenstein*. It was published in 1818.

BLOODTHIRSTY BIRD

KEEP AN EYE ON THE SKY! THIS MEAT-EATING BIRD SWOOPS DOWN ON ITS PREY FROM ABOVE. ONCE THE BIRD HAS A VICTIM IN ITS TALONS, THERE'S NO ESCAPE.

1. Draw the basic frame of the bird. Try to keep a nice flow to your lines.

2. Over your skeleton, draw in basic tubes and curves to give the creature shape.

3. Refine your line work, adding details such as muscles and feathers. Then pencil in the shadows.

4. Ink over the top of your pencil sketch, defining even more of the details.

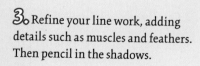

talon—a long, sharp claw

5. Color your drawing
with any colors you like.

WRAITH

THIS CREEPY GHOST HAS ONLY ONE MISSION—TO GET REVENGE FOR HIS DEATH. HIS OUTSTRETCHED ARMS GIVE THE DRAWING PERSPECTIVE. SHOW YOUR FRIENDS THIS GHASTLY GHOUL, AND THEY MIGHT JUMP BACK!

1. Begin by building a basic structure with simple shapes. Use circles to show joints in the body. Use cylinders and ovals to show limbs and larger elements. A cross helps define the center of the face. The arrows show the flow of the monster's clothing.

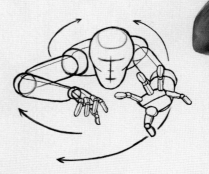

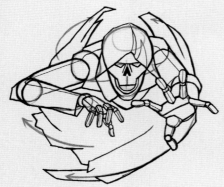

2. Start to add features to the skull and definition to the figure with straight lines. When drawing skeletons, a science book is often useful for drawing the parts correctly.

3. Refine the outline. When drawing limbs, think of their angle and perspective in relation to the viewer. The monster's left arm is outstretched, causing parts of the forearm to be hidden by the hand. The left hand is larger because it is much closer to the viewer than the other.

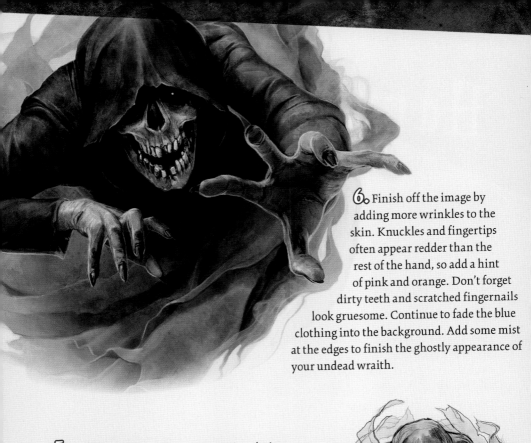

6. Finish off the image by adding more wrinkles to the skin. Knuckles and fingertips often appear redder than the rest of the hand, so add a hint of pink and orange. Don't forget dirty teeth and scratched fingernails look gruesome. Continue to fade the blue clothing into the background. Add some mist at the edges to finish the ghostly appearance of your undead wraith.

5. Continue shading your monster in relation to the light source. In this case, the light is coming from above. Notice how strong, dark shadows draw attention to the face. Also, the farther away the fabric is, the paler it becomes. Using contrast like this adds depth. The left hand is now really starting to reach out off the page.

4. Use your own hands as a reference when refining the monster's fingers. Make sure the hood and sleeves hang down with a convincing sense of weight. Soften the fabric using curved lines, and add layers in it to create interest and movement.

Harpy

IN GREEK MYTHS, HARPIES WERE FLYING BEASTS THAT CONSTANTLY STOLE FOOD FROM THRACIAN KING PHINEAS. THESE NASTY WINGED MONSTERS LIVE ON IN MODERN HORROR MOVIES AND BOOKS.

1. Start with a basic structure built from simple shapes. Use balls to show shoulders and other parts. Larger ovals can be used to show the head and torso.

2. Join your shapes together with straight lines and angular shapes. Begin to create the wing structure. Each wing has three layers. Add long primary feathers along the edges of the wings using straight lines.

3. Primary feathers at the tips of the wings are longest and splay out like fingers. Feathers closer to the body tend to be shorter and compact. There is only one row of large primary feathers. Give your monster a scary expression. Open the feet to display its deadly talons.

4. The **shaft** of a feather is almost straight, but the tip curves away from the body. Use overlapping curved lines to suggest layers of different-sized feathers. Large feathers form the bottom row and get smaller toward the top. Add feathery hair to complement the wings.

shaft—the central stem of a feather

6. Highlight the upper edge of the talons to suggest light hitting the monster from above. The stomach is in deep shadow because the head and shoulders are blocking the light. Yellow, jagged teeth, along with angry slanted brows, add gruesomeness and terror. Add a hint of yellow across the nose to resemble an eagle's beak. Specks of dirt flying off the monster show movement and an unclean nature.

5. Blend the humanoid head, chest, and shoulders into the bird parts. Shade your monster. Add shadow to the feathers closest to the body. This helps separate the shape of the torso from the wingspan.

Cerberus

THE CERBERUS IS A THREE-HEADED MONSTER FROM GREEK AND ROMAN MYTHS. THE HOUND FIERCELY GUARDED THE UNDERWORLD. THIS DRAWING PRESENTS THE CHALLENGE OF SHADING ACCORDING TO VARIOUS LIGHT SOURCES.

1. Begin by building a basic structure with simple shapes. Use balls to show joints in the skeleton, like knees and hips. Use differently sized ovals to show limbs and larger elements. Crosses help define the center of the faces and show which direction each head is looking.

2. Start adding features to the heads and defining the body parts with straight lines. Make sure the legs are posed correctly in relation to each other. Remember a dog's hind legs bend differently than human legs do.

3. Refine the outline and the places where the joints and limbs meet. The hind legs are farther away and should appear smaller. Some parts will be partially hidden behind others. Adjust the pose to be sure nothing is confusing.

4. After removing unwanted structure lines, determine the light source and add shadow to your monster.

Here, the fire is the light source, which is flowing from the monster's back. The underside of the body is in the darkest shadow because it is on the opposite side of the fire.

FACT: Some artwork shows the Cerberus with as many as 50 heads.

5. Continue to shade your monster. Focus on giving the body a three-dimensional appearance. Add details like wrinkles around the mouth and glaring eyes to give the drawing character. Use lines to suggest ribs and muscles protruding from beneath the skin.

CONTINUE NEXT PAGE

6. Use flat color to define different parts of your monster. You can now clearly see the shape of the red body against the orange fire. Add a solid floor for the monster to stand on, which helps give the monster a sense of weight.

7. Start to paint over and remove outlines to give your monster a more realistic appearance. Adding flames to the legs lights up the underside of the jaw and neck. This is called reflected light, and it's a key element when trying to capture realism and depth. Note how the torso is lit from the fire above and the lava from below. The darker skin in between helps provide a three-dimensional effect. The heads are also shaded in this way.

8. Areas in shadow often look colder. Add a hint of blue and gray to the areas farthest away from the bright, hot fire. The fire from within the monster's mouths and eyes adds a chilling quality. Think about how a new light source affects the area around it. In this case, parts of the mouth, the teeth, and the skin around the eyes are being lit up.

9. Hiding parts of the back legs with fire and smoke helps add **atmosphere** and more depth to the image. Cracks and lava in the floor help show the kind of environment the monster lives in. They also show how the monster's body affects the space around it. Elements like this help make the drawing more believable and add interest.

atmosphere—a mood or feeling created by a work of art

READ MORE

Beaumont, Steve. *Drawing Dragons and Other Cold-Blooded Creatures.* Drawing Legendary Monsters. New York: PowerKids Press, 2011.

Sautter, Aaron. *The Boys' Guide to Drawing Aliens, Warriors, Robots and Other Cool Stuff.* Mankato, Minn.: Capstone Press, 2009.

Temple, Kathryn. *Drawing in Color.* Art for Kids. New York: Lark Books, 2009.

INTERNET SITES

FactHound offers a safe, fun way to find Internet sites related to this book. All of the sites on FactHound have been researched by our staff.

Here's all you do:

Visit *www.facthound.com*

Type in this code: 9781429675383